BUILDING YOUR ARSENAL

ONE SCRIPTURE AT A TIME

GladysMarie Harris, Ph.D.

Copyright © 2023 GladysMarie Harris, LLC

All rights reserved. No part of this publication in print or in electronic format may be reproduced, stored in a retrieval system, or transmitted in any form or by any means, electronic, mechanical, photocopying, recording, or otherwise without the prior written permission of the publisher.

The scanning, uploading, and distribution of this book without permission is a theft of the author's intellectual property. Thank you for your support of the author's rights.

Design and distribution by Bublish
Published by GladysMarie W.R. Harris Publishing

ISBN: 978-1-647047-10-8 (paperback)

Thanks to my wonderful husband, A. Douglas Rogers, for his support and love throughout all my endeavors and adventures.

Spiritual warfare is all around. . . . Don't mistake it as something else.

Hosea 4:6 says, "My people are destroyed from lack of knowledge. . .".

So let's gain some knowledge!

WHY DO WE NEED AN "ARSENAL"?

In order to prepare for the battle, we as Christians must begin building our arsenal on a daily basis. What does that mean? Learn hand-to-hand combat, get a gun, visit the firing range daily or weekly, or never leave the house to expose yourself to danger? Unfortunately, the war that is waged on Christians cannot be fought using hand-to-hand combat or a gun, and if we decide to hide inside our homes, the war is still waged on each Christian. The war is waged in our minds, and we must be prepared to fight at that level. This book is designed to begin the pre-war stage for Christians to become equipped for battle in their mind.

I meet Christians on a daily basis, and I find that they have no weapons at all in their arsenals, so when they are confronted by the enemy, the enemy is prepared to win. Unfortunately, the enemy usually does win when you have no weapons to fight them.

Many Christians attempt to adopt worldly quotes as scriptures from the Bible, such as:

- Name it and claim it.
- God doesn't put any more on you than you can handle.

- If God has it for you, it'll always be there waiting for you.

This book begins the step of memorizing a few powerful verses to start preparing your arsenal so the next time the enemy shows up, you are prepared. As you memorize the scripture verses, you will have weapons to keep you sane that stand the test of time. The next time you encounter the overwhelming or unbelievable, first, pray for the correct verse to come to the forefront of your mind and second, know you are equipped to battle the enemy that has shown itself in your life.

There are so many scriptures throughout the Bible that can be used in your arsenal. The scriptures selected for this book have been very meaningful in my life. All scriptures are from the New King James Version unless otherwise noted. Weapons 21, 22 and 23 are scriptures that you choose to add to your personal arsenal.

CONTENTS

Arsenal of Weapons   Page No.

Weapon #1	John 10:10	2
Weapon #2	Psalm 18:2	4
Weapon #3	Luke 6:38	6
Weapon #4	Isaiah 40:31	8
Weapon #5	2 Corinthians 9:6	10
Weapon #6	Exodus 14:14	12
Weapon #7	Proverbs 22:7	14
Weapon #8	Hebrews 13:5	16
Weapon #9	John 14:14	18
Weapon #10	Proverbs 19:17	20
Weapon #11	Romans 13:8	22
Weapon #12	Psalm 23:4	24
Weapon #13	Numbers 30:2	26
Weapon #14	Hebrews 11:6	28
Weapon #15	Philippians 4:6	30
Weapon #16	Matthew 5:16	32
Weapon #17	Matthew 25:35–36 and 40	34
Weapon #18	Isaiah 43:2	36
Weapon #19	Matthew 4:4	38
Weapon #20	Psalm 27:1	40
Weapon #21	_____	42
Weapon #22	_____	43
Weapon #23	_____	44

Index 47

WEAPON #1

The first weapon is *John 10:10*. This scripture addresses how we can identify the enemy when he enters our life, mind, and plans.

LET'S MEMORIZE

John 10:10 says,

> The thief does not come except to steal, and to kill, and to destroy. I [Jesus] have come that they may have life, and that they may have it more abundantly.

WHEN TO USE THIS SCRIPTURE

Have you ever had plans to complete a task or project but so many roadblocks and obstacles attempt to stop you? Does doubt come to mind? This is when you need to repeat this scripture and remind yourself that the enemy wants to steal, kill, and destroy what you're doing. Remember, Jesus came so you may have life and have it more abundantly.

INSTRUCTIONS

Repeat the scripture seven (7) times out loud. Close your eyes and see the words in your mind as you say them out loud. Write the scripture in your mind and heart.

For the next week, repeat the scripture seven times every morning, midday, and in the evening. During the course of the week, if you encounter someone or something attempting to steal, kill, or destroy what you are doing, acknowledge the thief. You can only defeat the enemy if you know the enemy's characteristics.

WRITE THE VERSE BELOW

WEAPON #2

The second weapon is *Psalm 18:2*. This scripture addresses the strength and might of our Lord in our life.

LET'S MEMORIZE

Psalm 18:2 says,

> The Lord is my rock and my fortress and my deliverer; My God, my extra strength, in whom I will trust; My shield and the horn of my salvation, my stronghold.

WHEN TO USE THIS SCRIPTURE

When you're feeling vulnerable, or everything is spinning out of control. This scripture will give you peace of mind that God is in control, and everything will be all right, even though you cannot control the outcome.

• INSTRUCTIONS

Repeat the scripture seven (7) times out loud. Close your eyes and see the words in your mind as you say them out loud. Write the scripture in your mind and heart. Repeat any prior scripture(s) at least one time each day.

For the next week, repeat the scripture seven times every morning, midday, and in the evening. During the course of the week, if you feel vulnerable, repeat the scripture to yourself.

WRITE THE VERSE BELOW

WEAPON #3

The third weapon is *Luke 6:38*. This scripture encourages a person to have a humble heart and to give of their belongings and finances.

LET'S MEMORIZE

Luke 6:38 says,

> Give, and it will be given to you. A good measure, pressed down, shaken together and running over, will be poured into your lap. For with the measure you use, it will be measured to you.

WHEN TO USE THIS SCRIPTURE

It is easy to hold on to money and possessions when you don't believe you will ever get them again; however, God gives us more than enough and expects you to share. Remember this scripture when giving because what you give will be the way God measures what you will receive.

INSTRUCTIONS

Repeat the scripture seven (7) times out loud. Close your eyes and see the words in your mind as you say them. Write the scripture in your mind and heart. Repeat any prior scripture(s) at least one time each day.

For the next week, repeat the scripture seven times every morning, midday, and in the evening. During the week, if you encounter a situation in which you can give to someone, remember that how you give is also how you will be measured in receiving.

WRITE THE VERSE BELOW

WEAPON #4

The fourth weapon is *Isaiah 40:31*. This scripture addresses how waiting for the Lord will allow you to renew your energy.

LET'S MEMORIZE

Isaiah 40:31 says,

> But those who wait on the Lord shall renew their strength; They shall mount up with wings like eagles, They shall run and not be weary, They shall walk and not faint.

WHEN TO USE THIS SCRIPTURE

You should never be anxious over anything—instead, wait on the Lord to move. This is easier to say than to do, but for those who wait, everything will be renewed.

INSTRUCTIONS

Repeat the scripture seven (7) times out loud. Close your eyes and see the words in your mind as you say them. Write the scripture in your mind and heart. Repeat any prior scripture(s) at least one time each day.

For the next week, repeat the scripture seven times every morning, midday, and in the evening. During the course of the week, if you encounter a problem, pray and wait upon the Lord.

WRITE THE VERSE BELOW

WEAPON #5

The fifth weapon is *2 Corinthians 9:6*. This scripture addresses what you will receive from the fruits of your labor.

LET'S MEMORIZE

2 Corinthians 9:6 says,

> Remember this: Whoever sows sparingly will also reap sparingly, and whoever sows generously will also reap generously.

WHEN TO USE THIS SCRIPTURE

If you are completing a task/project/goal and a little of your time is given to it, you will receive little success. When a generous amount of your time is given, you will have a generous result.

INSTRUCTIONS

Repeat the scripture seven (7) times out loud. Close your eyes and see the words in your mind as you say them. Write the scripture in your mind and heart. Repeat any prior scripture(s) at least one time each day.

For the next week, repeat the scripture seven times every morning, midday, and in the evening. During the course of the week, remember to do exceptional work because if you do less than exceptionally, you will get a less-than-exceptional reward.

WRITE THE VERSE BELOW

....

....

....

....

....

....

....

WEAPON #6

The sixth weapon is *Exodus 14:14*. This scripture addresses how you should let the Lord fight your battles.

LET'S MEMORIZE

Exodus 14:14 says,

> The Lord will fight for you; you need only to be still.

WHEN TO USE THIS SCRIPTURE

When you feel that war is breaking out against you, remember that the battle is not yours to fight. You need to let the Lord fight and simply be still and stand. Instead of fighting, pray and repeat this scripture.

INSTRUCTIONS

Repeat the scripture seven (7) times out loud. Close your eyes and see the words in your mind as you say them. Write the scripture in your mind and heart. Repeat any prior scripture(s) at least one time each day.

For the next week, repeat the scripture seven times every morning, midday, and in the evening. During the course of the week, if you encounter a battle, repeat the scripture to yourself and just stand still.

WRITE THE VERSE BELOW

....

....

....

....

....

....

....

WEAPON #7

The seventh weapon is **_Proverbs 22:7_**. This scripture addresses how you should stay within your budget and avoid borrowing.

LET'S MEMORIZE

Proverbs 22:7 says,

> The rich rule over the poor, and the borrower is servant to the lender.

WHEN TO USE THIS SCRIPTURE

When you are in need of material possessions, remember to not go into debt unless you want to be a servant (slave) to the lender. The lender has total control. They can increase rates on credit cards or mature loans without a reason and without the agreement of the borrower.

INSTRUCTIONS

Repeat the scripture seven (7) times out loud. Close your eyes and see the words in your mind as you say them. Write the scripture in your mind and heart. Repeat any prior scripture(s) at least one time each day.

For the next week, repeat the scripture seven times every morning, midday, and in the evening. During the course of the week, if you are tempted to go outside your budget to buy something you cannot afford, repeat the scripture to yourself.

WRITE THE VERSE BELOW

....

....

....

....

....

....

....

WEAPON #8

The eighth weapon is *Hebrews 13:5*. This scripture addresses being grateful for what you have and how God will never leave or forsake you.

LET'S MEMORIZE

Hebrews 13:5 says,

> Keep your lives free from the love of money and be content with what you have, because God has said, "Never will I leave you; never will I forsake you."

WHEN TO USE THIS SCRIPTURE

Don't let money drive you every day and every evening. The love of money or greed will destroy you. God said He will never leave or forsake you if you are free of the love of money. Be content with what God has given you.

INSTRUCTIONS

Repeat the scripture seven (7) times out loud. Close your eyes and see the words in your mind as you say them. Write the scripture in your mind and heart. Repeat any prior scripture(s) at least one time each day.

For the next week, repeat the scripture seven times every morning, midday, and in the evening. During the course of the week, if you find yourself not being happy with what you have, repeat the scripture to yourself.

WRITE THE VERSE BELOW

WEAPON #9

The ninth weapon is *John 14:14*. This scripture addresses how you can ask for anything in the name of Jesus, and he will hear and do it.

LET'S MEMORIZE

John 14:14 says,

> If you ask anything in My name, I will do it.

WHEN TO USE THIS SCRIPTURE

If you are in need, remember anything that is asked in Jesus's name will be given unto you; however, it will be in God's time. If you are not prepared to handle what you are requesting, it will not be given.

INSTRUCTIONS

Repeat the scripture seven (7) times out loud. Close your eyes and see the words in your mind as you say them. Write the scripture in your mind and heart. Repeat any prior scripture(s) at least one time each day.

For the next week, repeat the scripture seven times every morning, midday, and in the evening. During the course of the week, if you are in need of anything, ask it in Jesus's name.

WRITE THE VERSE BELOW

....

....

....

....

....

....

....

....

WEAPON #10

The tenth weapon is **Proverbs 19:17**. This scripture addresses how we should treat the poor.

LET'S MEMORIZE

Proverbs 19:17 says,

> Whoever is kind to the poor lends to the Lord, and he will reward them for what they have done.

WHEN TO USE THIS SCRIPTURE

When you encounter the poor and your spirit moves you to help or give, remember that what you give is being given to the Lord, and you will be rewarded for what you have done.

• INSTRUCTIONS

Repeat the scripture seven (7) times out loud. Close your eyes and see the words in your mind as you say them. Write the scripture in your mind and heart. Repeat any prior scripture(s) at least one time each day.

For the next week, repeat the scripture seven times every morning, midday, and in the evening. During the course of the week, if you encounter someone in need and you lend to them, you are also lending to the Lord, and you will be rewarded.

WRITE THE VERSE BELOW

WEAPON #11

The eleventh weapon is **Romans 13:8**. This scripture addresses paying all your outstanding debts except the debt to love one another.

LET'S MEMORIZE

Romans 13:8 says,

> Let no debt remain outstanding, except the continuing debt to love one another, for whoever loves others has fulfilled the law.

WHEN TO USE THIS SCRIPTURE

Remember, there should never be any outstanding debts owed except the debt to love one another. The debt to love one another will never be paid in full.

INSTRUCTIONS

Repeat the scripture seven (7) times out loud. Close your eyes and see the words in your mind as you say them. Write the scripture in your mind and heart. Repeat any prior scripture(s) at least one time each day.

For the next week, repeat the scripture every morning, midday, and in the evening seven times. During the course of the week, remember to eliminate your debt unless it is debt of love to one another.

WRITE THE VERSE BELOW

WEAPON #12

The twelfth weapon is *Psalm 23:4*. This scripture addresses comfort when you're going through a troubled time.

LET'S MEMORIZE

Psalm 23:4 says,

> Yea, though I walk through the valley of the shadow of death, I will fear no evil; For You are with me; Your rod and Your staff, they comfort me.

WHEN TO USE THIS SCRIPTURE

We all have those bad days, troubled times, and disappointments that happen in life. This scripture allows you to know there is no need to fear, and God's rod and staff will comfort you while you're going through those times. You are not alone. You are never alone.

INSTRUCTIONS

Repeat the scripture seven (7) times out loud. Close your eyes and see the words in your mind as you say them. Write the scripture in your mind and heart. Repeat any prior scripture(s) at least one time each day.

For the next week, repeat the scripture every morning, midday and in the evening seven times. During the course of the week, if you encounter fear or anxiety, repeat the scripture to yourself.

WRITE THE VERSE BELOW

....

....

....

....

....

....

....

....

WEAPON #13

The thirteenth weapon is *Numbers 30:2*. This scripture addresses how a commitment to the Lord is sacred and must be completed.

LET'S MEMORIZE

Numbers 30:2 says,

> If a man makes a vow to the Lord, or swears an oath to bind himself by some agreement, he shall not break his word; he shall do according to all that proceeds out of his mouth.

WHEN TO USE THIS SCRIPTURE

When you make a vow or commitment, you must make sure you do not break your word because the vow was made before the Lord.

INSTRUCTIONS

Repeat the scripture seven (7) times out loud. Close your eyes and see the words in your mind as you say them. Write the scripture in your mind and heart. Repeat any prior scripture(s) at least one time each day.

For the next week, repeat the scripture every morning, midday, and in the evening seven times. During the course of the week, remember not to break any vow you make to the Lord.

WRITE THE VERSE BELOW

WEAPON #14

The fourteenth weapon is *Hebrews 11:6*. This scripture addresses how you can please God.

LET'S MEMORIZE

Hebrews 11:6 says,

> And without faith it is impossible to please God, because anyone who comes to him must believe that he exists and that he rewards those who earnestly seek him.

WHEN TO USE THIS SCRIPTURE

Have you been concerned about how to please God? Do you believe you must pray multiple times a day? Participating in such religious traditions as communion, attending church multiple times a week, or becoming a minister are not the way to please God. Having faith that He exists and seeking Him throughout your day is how to please God.

INSTRUCTIONS

Repeat the scripture seven (7) times out loud. Close your eyes and see the words in your mind as you say them. Write the scripture in your mind and heart. Repeat any prior scripture(s) at least one time each day.

For the next week, repeat the scripture every morning, midday, and in the evening seven times. During the course of the week, remember you don't need to please anyone except God and repeat the scripture to yourself.

WRITE THE VERSE BELOW

WEAPON #15

The fifteenth weapon is *Philippians 4:6*. This scripture addresses not being anxious about anything but using prayer and petitioning to God with thanksgiving for all concerns.

LET'S MEMORIZE

Philippians 4:6 says,

> Do not be anxious about anything, but in every situation, by prayer and petition, with thanksgiving, present your requests to God.

WHEN TO USE THIS SCRIPTURE

Use this scripture when you feel overwhelmed or anxious about a situation or concern. Remember to take everything to God in prayer and petition with thanksgiving.

INSTRUCTIONS

Repeat the scripture seven (7) times out loud. Close your eyes and see the words in your mind as you say them. Write the scripture in your mind and heart. Repeat any prior scripture(s) at least one time each day.

For the next week, repeat the scripture every morning, midday, and in the evening seven times. During the course of the week, remember to ask God for everything you need and want through prayer.

WRITE THE VERSE BELOW

WEAPON #16

The sixteenth weapon is *Matthew 5:16*. This scripture addresses how you should glorify your Father in heaven.

LET'S MEMORIZE

Matthew 5:16 says,

> Let your light shine before men, that they may see your good works and glorify your Father in heaven.

WHEN TO USE THIS SCRIPTURE

When doing a good deed or working on a task or project that will assist others, let your light shine like a beacon in the dark, and this will glorify your Father in heaven.

INSTRUCTIONS

Repeat the scripture seven (7) times out loud. Close your eyes and see the words in your mind as you say them. Write the scripture in your mind and heart. Repeat any prior scripture(s) at least one time each day.

For the next week, repeat the scripture every morning, midday, and in the evening seven times. During the course of the week, when you do good, remember that others see your actions. Repeat the scripture to yourself.

WRITE THE VERSE BELOW

WEAPON #17

The seventeenth weapon is *Matthew 25:35–36 and 40* (NIV). This scripture addresses how you should treat your brothers and sisters in life.

LET'S MEMORIZE

Matthew 25:35–36 and 40 say,

> For I was hungry and you gave me something to eat, I was thirsty and you gave me something to drink, I was a stranger and you invited me in, I needed clothes and you clothed me, I was sick and you looked after me, I was in prison and you came to visit me.
>
> ". . . Truly I tell you, whatever you did for one of the least of these brothers and sisters of mine, you did for me.

WHEN TO USE THIS SCRIPTURE

When you see others hungry, thirsty, naked, sick, or in prison or a stranger needing help, you should assist them in their need.

INSTRUCTIONS

Repeat the scripture seven (7) times out loud. Close your eyes and see the words in your mind as you say them. Write the scripture in your mind and heart. Repeat any prior scripture(s) at least one time each day.

For the next week, repeat the scripture every morning, midday, and in the evening seven times. During the course of the week, if you encounter someone in need of food, drink, or clothing or someone who is a stranger, in prison, or sick and you are able to help, then do so while repeating the scripture to yourself.

WRITE THE VERSE BELOW

WEAPON #18

The eighteenth weapon is *Isaiah 43:2*. This scripture addresses God's strength and comfort when you are going through trouble that you believe is unbearable.

LET'S MEMORIZE

Isaiah 43:2 says,

> When you pass through the waters, God will be with you; and when you pass through the rivers, they will not sweep over you. When you walk through the fire, you will not be burned; the flames will not set you ablaze.

WHEN TO USE THIS SCRIPTURE

You're not the only one who encounters trouble, hardship, and disappointment in life, and on many occasions, it seems overwhelming. This scripture will give you comfort in knowing that you will survive and live another day.

INSTRUCTIONS

Repeat the scripture seven (7) times out loud. Close your eyes and see the words in your mind as you say them. Write the scripture in your mind and heart. Repeat any prior scripture(s) at least one time each day.

For the next week, repeat the scripture every morning, midday, and in the evening seven times. During the course of the week, if you encounter a difficult time or situation, repeat the scripture to yourself.

WRITE THE VERSE BELOW

WEAPON #19

The nineteenth weapon is *Matthew 4:4* (NIV). This scripture addresses relying on every word out of the mouth of God.

LET'S MEMORIZE

Matthew 4:4 says,

> It is written that "Man shall not live on bread alone, but on every word that comes from the mouth of God."

WHEN TO USE THIS SCRIPTURE

When trouble appears in your life, remember to pacify yourself with the word of God, not food. Start repeating a memorized scripture to feed your soul.

INSTRUCTIONS

Repeat the scripture seven (7) times out loud. Close your eyes and see the words in your mind as you say them. Write the scripture in your mind and heart. Repeat any prior scripture(s) at least one time each day.

For the next week, repeat the scripture every morning, midday, and in the evening seven times. During the course of the week, remember we rely on every word that comes out of the mouth of God.

WRITE THE VERSE BELOW

WEAPON #20

The twentieth weapon is **Psalm 27:1**. This scripture addresses the issue of not being fearful and why.

LET'S MEMORIZE

Psalm 27:1 says,

> The Lord is my light and my salvation. Whom shall I fear? The Lord is the strength of my life. Of whom shall I be afraid?

WHEN TO USE THIS SCRIPTURE

When you feel fearful in any situation, you should start repeating this scripture. There is nothing too big for God to handle, so why should you ever fear anything? Nothing surprises God, so why be afraid?

INSTRUCTIONS

Repeat the scripture seven (7) times out loud. Close your eyes and see the words in your mind as you say them. Write the scripture in your mind and heart. Repeat any prior scripture(s) at least one time each day.

For the next week, repeat the scripture every morning, midday, and in the evening seven times. During the course of the week, if you feel fearful or afraid, repeat the scripture to yourself.

WRITE THE VERSE BELOW

....

....

....

....

....

....

....

....

WEAPON #21

SCRIPTURE

WHEN WILL YOU USE THIS SCRIPTURE?

WEAPON #22

SCRIPTURE

WHEN WILL YOU USE THIS SCRIPTURE?

WEAPON #23

SCRIPTURE

WHEN WILL YOU USE THIS SCRIPTURE?

THOUGHTS

THOUGHTS

INDEX

Scripture	Page
2 Corinthians 9:6	10
Exodus 14:14	12
Hebrews 11:6	28
Hebrews 13:5	16
Isaiah 40:31	8
Isaiah 43:2	36
John 10:10	2
John 14:14	18
Luke 6:38	6
Matthew 4:4	38
Matthew 5:16	32
Matthew 25:35–36 & 40	34
Numbers 30:2	26
Philippians 4:6	30
Proverbs 19:17	20
Proverbs 22:7	14
Psalm 18:2	4
Psalm 23:4	24
Psalm 27:1	40
Romans 13:8	22

www.ingramcontent.com/pod-product-compliance
Lightning Source LLC
Chambersburg PA
CBHW071917070526
44583CB00016B/2025